Praying With O

Greg Hildenbrand

Praying With One Eye Open

Greg Hildenbrand

Greg Hildenbrand

Copyright © 2019 Hildenbrand

All rights gently reserved. Except as permitted under the U.S. Copyright Act of 1976, no part of this publication may be reproduced, distributed, or transmitted in any form or by any means, or stored in a database or retrieval system without prior written permission of the author (unless the reader has an altruistic reason for doing so).

Additional information, books, music, podcasts, and other resources are available at www.ContemplatingGrace.com

ISBN-13: 9781696709538

Also by Greg Hildenbrand

Books
Finding Grace in an Imperfect World (2014)
Finding Grace in Lent (2015)
Uncovering God in Christmas (2015)
Paul Wrote the Book of Love (2016)
How Did I Miss That? (2017)
The Faces of God (2018)
What Jesus Said (2018)
A Contemplative Life (2019)

Music CDs
Finding Grace in an Imperfect World (2014)
Songs of Lent (2015)
Songs of Christmas (2015)
Questions of Being (2018)

Additional information and to order:
www.ContemplatingGrace.com

CONTENTS

	Preface	1
1	Praying With One Eye Open	3
2	Trusting Divine Provision	7
3	Treasure in Heaven	10
4	Staying Awake	13
5	Lukewarm Living	17
6	The Redeeming Face of Love	21
7	The Sign of Jonah	25
8	The Exodus Revisited	29
9	Bits and Bytes	33
10	Silent Prayer	37
11	Praying Together	41
12	Walking Prayer	45
13	Fear and Awe	49

14	Praying the Details	53
15	The Second Arrow	56
16	Dealing With Dharma	60
17	A Den of Thieves	64
18	Difficult Decisions	68
19	A Beautiful Soul, Part 1	72
20	A Beautiful Soul, Part 2	76
21	A Beautiful Soul, Part 3	80
22	God's I Do Not Believe In	84
23	Divine Violence, Part 1	88
24	Divine Violence, Part 2	92
25	Divine Violence, Part 3	96
26	Praying With Both Eyes Closed	100
27	Praying With One Eye Open (Reprise)	103
	Appendix A: Intro to Centering Prayer	107
	Appendix B: Intro to Lectio Divina	110
	Appendix C: Intro to Meditative Walking	112
	About the Author	115

Greg Hildenbrand

Preface

Too often, I find myself living life as a whirling dervish, allowing myself to be pushed and pulled in many different directions at once. My home office is full of partially completed books and music. My yard has a number of projects in various states of becoming. Some of my important relationships have issues left open. I often say there are not enough hours in a day to complete the tasks on my plate, but I know that is not true. The problem is my lack of focus and presence on the task and life before me at any given time.

In the following pages, I refer to a lack of focused attention as *praying with one eye open*. It is neither bad nor uncommon to attempt to multi-task our way through our *to-do* lists, and sometimes that is a necessary reality. Most of the time, however, at least for me, attempting to multi-task is not a necessity but a symptom of my lack of focus.

The bulk of this book attempts to help identify the forces that pull us out of the moment, as well as providing strategies for returning to it. The appendices provide tools to aid in the process. My prayer is that you and I can find our way back to the beautiful and expansive moment where all of life is happening all of the time.

Greg Hildenbrand
October 2019

Greg Hildenbrand

Chapter 1

Praying With One Eye Open

You shall not make for yourself an idol. You shall not bow down to them or worship them; for I the LORD your God am a jealous God. Exodus 20:4a,5a,b

The book of Exodus records Moses' visits with God on Mount Sinai. On one of those visits, God gives Moses the Ten Commandments. One of those commandments warns against making idols for ourselves because *God is a jealous God*. I always found this particular commandment troubling because of the description of God as jealous. Jealousy seems too petty for an all-powerful, all-loving God. I remember jealousy as the product of teenage hormones running wild, combined with insecurity and immaturity. Jealousy was ugly, hurtful, and certainly not befitting of God. Besides, what could possibly make God jealous of us?

Based on my nebulous experiences of God over the years, I think using the contemporary understanding of jealousy is misleading. God's jealousy, in part, has to do with our free will. No one wants love forced upon them, nor does anyone want to be loved because another feels sorry for or obligated to love him or her. That is charity, not love.

Deep love is always offered but never imposed. We can accept God's love or not. God's love for us does not diminish because we refuse to acknowledge or reciprocate it. Jesus' parable of the Prodigal Son (Luke 15:11-31) illustrates the point well. The younger son turns away from his father, but the father's love

God seldom comes to us as a thunderbolt, but as the wind whispering gently through the trees or a hummingbird visiting the honeysuckle.

for his wayward son never wavers. God does not turn from us like a jealous, spurned lover; rather, we miss God's reaching out to us because we are focused elsewhere.

God is described as jealous because *our experience* of God is fickle. We are so wrapped up in our earthly existence that encounters with God are difficult to recognize. Such experiences are usually subtle and easily missed when we are not paying attention. God seldom comes to us as a thunderbolt, but as the wind whispering gently through the trees or a hummingbird visiting the honeysuckle. Paying attention to God and seeking God's presence is difficult with our endless opportunities for distraction. Our modern-day idols are not carved images of animals or pagan gods, but are our addictions, smart phones, social media, and television – things that keep us out of a deep experience with the present moment. Our seductive idols draw our attention away from rich encounters with loved ones, including our experiences of God's love. God is not jealous because we spend so much time with the objects of our obsessions. Rather, God hurts because our obsessions keep us from being aware of God's nearness, which hurts us. God hurts *for* us, not because of us. It is not so much God's heart that breaks, but ours that would break if we knew what we were giving up for the temporary high of an idolatrous encounter. There is no permanence or security in our distractions, only a diversion from what matters most.

Lest this sound like a holier-than-thou, guilt-imposing diatribe, I confess my own on-going tendency toward diversion from the present moment. I *know* I cannot experience God anywhere or anytime other than *right here* and *right now*, but I struggle mightily with sincerely seeking God on a more than infrequent basis. That is part of our human nature and not cause for guilt or self-deprecation. Rather, it is an opportunity for spiritual growth. God waits patiently for us, as did the prodigal's father, and in the context of eternity, there is no particular rush. Our very human obligations prevent us from focusing on God in every waking moment, anyway. It is comforting to know, however, that God is accessible should we need a divine encounter.

Praying with one eye open is a metaphor for not giving oneself fully to God. When we close both eyes to pray, even for a short time, we make ourselves uncomfortably vulnerable – danger could approach that we would not see. We could miss something we want to see – like praying in front of a televised sporting event. Someone might notice and think less of us. Our addiction to earthly affairs causes us to keep an eye open, even though we know we cannot fully give ourselves over to God without loosening the grip our material interests hold over us. God speaks most often in silence and darkness. God's still small voice cannot be heard over the commotion of our lives, nor will God's presence draw our attention away from Facebook. God knows we need to turn away from our idols on occasion, close *both* eyes, and rest in the loving presence of the Divine.

Chapter 2

Trusting Divine Provision

When they hand you over, do not worry about how you are to speak or what you are to say; for what you are to say will be given to you at that time; for it is not you who speak, but the Spirit of your Father speaking through you.
Matthew 10:19-20

In this passage from Matthew, Jesus talks to his disciples about how to handle persecution. He tells them they do not need to prepare what they will say – how they will defend themselves – ahead of time, for that guidance will be provided to them at the necessary time. The consequences of persecution in Jesus' day were dire, compared to what most of us experience today, at least in the West. In Jesus' day, persecution for unacceptable beliefs or behaviors could lead to a wretched death, as evidenced by Jesus' crucifixion.

Jesus frequently warns against worrying about future events. For example, in Luke 12:22, he says, "Do not worry about your life, what you will eat, or about your body, what you will wear." He emphasizes that life is much more than the things about which we worry. Worry is *always* future-oriented, but life only occurs in the present moment. It is not that food, clothing, shelter, and our responses to others are not important, but that it is God who assures the meeting of our needs *as the needs arise*. Jesus reminds us that God knows our needs. We become anxious when we suspect we *might* need something in the future and fret because we do not have it *now*. In the context of persecution, why waste time and energy formulating a response before we know a response will even be required? We only get caught up an a whirlpool of negative thoughts and emotions that have no substance.

Jesus seems to be saying that worrying about a possible future need is like praying with one eye open – it is evidence of our lack of faith and trust in God's provision. *What you are to say will be given to you at that time*. Why? Because *it is not you who speak, but the Spirit*

***We become anxious when we suspect we* might *need something in the future and fret because we do not have it* now.**

---

of your Father speaking through you. God lives and works in and through us in *all* circumstances. We cannot keep one eye focused on God while the other gazes into the future. It is not that Jesus discourages us from planning for the future; rather, Jesus tells us not *worry* about the future. Worry helps nothing. We have everything we need in any given moment, which should reassure us that we will have whatever we need in our future moments. We absolutely should select a path to follow into the future, understanding that all paths are fraught with difficulty and uncertainty. The future, however, is never in doubt, even though it may not unfold as we envision.

It is a natural tendency for us to want to be in control and plan for future eventualities. Unfortunately (or fortunately), we are not in control. In fact, I think anytime we try to be overly controlling, the universe objects and arranges something to show us how little control we actually have over events. Obsessing over the future only removes us from the present moment, which is the only place we can actually find joy. There are few savings accounts large enough to pay for a serious health crisis; there are few homes strong enough to survive a direct hit from a tornado; no one is safe from a terrorist attack anywhere on earth. Far from a license to live recklessly or with no thought of the future, the reality is that life sometimes brings unexpected and unplanned-for disasters, and God can be trusted for the recovery from those disasters, large and small. In the Lord's Prayer, we ask for our "daily bread." We do not ask for tomorrow's bread until tomorrow.

When we live our lives as if we are praying with one eye open, we live without faith in God's provision for our needs *at the time of the need.* Jesus assures us that God can be trusted to provide – maybe not in the manner or timeframe we desire, but God will provide. We can close both eyes, relax, enter the moment, and trust the Divine provision. Admittedly, however, not to pray with one eye open – hedging our bets against God's provision – is easier to say than to do.

Chapter 3

Treasure in Heaven

Jesus, looking at him, loved him and said, "You lack one thing; go, sell what you own, and give the money to the poor, and you will have treasure in heaven; then come, follow me."
Mark 10:21

In this story from Mark, a man asks Jesus what he must do to enter heaven. The man says he has kept all the commandments since his youth. Jesus says the man *still* lacks one thing – he must sell everything he owns and give the money to the poor. "When he heard this, (the man) was shocked and went away grieving, for he had many possessions." (Mark 10:22).

This story is interesting and discouraging. First, the man believed that following the commandments was what was required to enter heaven (as if we could *earn* our way into that state of grace). Turns out, he was wrong. I daresay, many of us today believe the same thing. Entering heaven is not about following rules, however, but about following the person of Christ, as modeled by Jesus of Nazareth. Following the commandments may be the result of our commitment to follow Christ, but they are not an end to themselves. In other words, the rules are not the goal; the orientation of our heart is the goal.

A second point, discouraging for many of us, is that we cannot have treasure on earth *and* treasure in heaven, at least not at the same time. To the extent that our possessions possess and encumber us, we cannot enter the kingdom of heaven. Our attachment to earthly things inhibits the freedom to follow Christ with our whole being. When we devote our time and

---

We cannot devote ourselves to two different and mutually exclusive causes at the same time. We must make a choice – one or the other.

---

resources to caring for and adding to our *stuff,* we cannot devote the time and resources available to us to serve others. Serving others in need was the sole focus of Jesus' life on earth. We cannot devote ourselves to two different and mutually exclusive causes at the same time. We must make a choice – one or the other. In the story, the man is shocked and grieved because he had many possessions. So am I, because so do I.

A third interesting and perplexing aspect of this story is that Jesus is NOT talking about heaven as a destination after this life is over. Jesus speaks about the kingdom of heaven as a *present* reality. The concept of heaven as an after-death destination is a relatively recent theological interpretation. Jesus says things like, "The kingdom of heaven is at hand," and "The kingdom of heaven is near." In the current story, Jesus indicates that once the man sells his possessions and gives the money to the poor, *at that time* he will have "treasure in heaven." The man is then to go to Jesus and follow him. It is all *present life*.

The more I carefully study Jesus, the more I realize he is *hard-core* about serving the less fortunate. I fear we soften his message in order to allow ourselves to feel holier. Most of us in the West make up the wealthiest of the world's citizens at any time in history. We live well beyond what is required to sustain our lives comfortably. While there is nothing unholy about living a comfortable life, the countless brothers and sisters across the globe lacking the most basic necessities to sustain life should at least concern us. Jesus gave everything he had, including his life, so others could live. Does entering heaven require us to do the same? Of course, our physical death will force the release of our material attachments. Our decision is whether to wait for death before releasing at least some of them.

Make no mistake, I have no plans to sell everything I own and give it to the poor. It is proof that I pray with one eye open, not fully trusting in God's provision for me. My challenge, and I believe yours, too, is to consciously consider my options with the resources I have at my disposal; if not all, then at least some. If I choose to buy another guitar, making me happy for a time, I simultaneously withhold resources that could relieve the suffering of another for a time. It is my choice. The story of the rich man in Mark is our story. One way to heaven is to keep both eyes closed in prayer – trusting in God – but both eyes open to the needs of those around us.

Chapter 4

Staying Awake

Keep awake and pray that you may not come into the time of trial; the spirit indeed is willing, but the flesh is weak.
Mark 14:38

Mindfulness is a popular buzzword these days. Be present to the moment. Be here now. Seize the day. We have many contemporary ways of saying what Jesus told his disciples 2000 years ago – *keep awake!* In the scripture from Mark, quoted above, Jesus is in the garden of Gethsemane with a few of his disciples after the Last Supper. He goes off by himself to pray and tells his friends to stay awake. He returns a short while later to find them asleep. He wakes them and again requests that they remain awake. Once again he goes off to pray, coming back a third time to find them asleep. At this point, the temple police have arrived to arrest him and begin the events that led to his crucifixion the next morning. In the context of this story, we are the sleepy disciples.

I do not believe Jesus asked his disciples to stay awake because he was lonely. He did not make the request so they would protect or hide him from his imminent fate. Rather, he wanted them to witness what was happening in the moment, to be present to it and *see* it, to *keep awake* to the details of what was happening around them. It was a seminal moment for each of them, personally and collectively, and he wanted them to experience it in the fullness of their being. One of the lessons we learn from difficult times is that we must go *through* our challenges in order to grow beyond them. To go through something requires that we be unwaveringly present

---

One of the lessons we learn from difficult times is that we must go* through *our challenges in order to grow beyond them.

---

to it, whatever it is. When we seek to avoid an experience, we automatically set the wheels in motion for a repeat occurrence. Only when we have acknowledged and accepted what is before us can we move on to something new. In order to acknowledge and accept what is, we must be awake.

Obviously, Jesus is not suggesting we stop sleeping. Rather, Jesus reminds us to pay attention during our waking hours – to the beauty around us, yes, but also to those people and events we find unpleasant, undesirable, or painful. Jesus understands how difficult it is for us; after all, he was human, too. While the text suggests his frustration with the disciples' inability to stay physically awake for his last moments of freedom on earth, he knows and verbalizes that the "flesh is weak." In spite of its inherent willingness, the spirit cannot override the tired flesh, at least not for long. The needs of the flesh are too powerful.

We stay awake, we become present to the moment by paying close attention to the information coming through our senses – what our eyes see and our ears hear. Jesus often pointed something out for his followers to examine, saying "Let those with eyes see." Many of his healing episodes involve blindness – physical blindness, yes, but these stories are also metaphorical pointers a more widespread type of blindness to whatever is before us. Opening ourselves to the full experience of what we see, hear, taste, touch, and smell unlocks the doorway into the present moment. Daydreaming about the future and regretting the past are fast-pass tickets out of the present, as is avoiding what we know requires our attention.

Taking ourselves out of the moment by any of the myriad of enticing ways to do so is like praying with one eye open. We tend not to trust the goodness or completeness of the moment any more than we trust God to protect and provide for us. As a result, we keep one eye open when we pray, and we avert our gaze from the present with an endless stream of diversions. Human nature, being what it is, makes it difficult *not* to do that! Jesus, however, calls us to transcend our ordinary human nature, not because there is anything wrong with being human, but because our human moments are beautiful, intense, intimate, and rich. Not only do we miss those powerful experiences when we stray from the moment, but God, experiencing through us, does as well. These experiences are only available in human bodies, so it is doubly important to embrace them as the opportunities arise. Jesus' admonition to keep awake is an invitation to fully experience our humanity, savoring and living every beautiful and painful moment while we are able to do so.

Chapter 5

Lukewarm Living

I know your words; you are neither cold nor hot. I wish that you were either cold or hot. So, because you are lukewarm, and neither cold nor hot, I am about to spit you out of my mouth.
Revelation 3:15-16

The author of the Revelation to John received messages for each of the seven churches in Asia at the time (present day Turkey). Some of the messages contain praise for their good works. All the messages contain criticism, some particularly harsh. The message to the church in Laodicea falls into the latter category. If one assumes, as I do, that scripture contains lessons for us as individuals, the criticism of the church at Laodicea hits me hard. This particular church is accused of being "lukewarm," which I interpret to mean disengaged. There was no passion or life in their worship or practice. The message says, "I wish that you were either cold or hot..." This church would be better off doing wrong things with zeal than doing right things without spirit. Because of this, Christ is about to spit them out of his mouth – to cast them away.

This message is vexing to me because I tend not to be emotionally expressive. The term *lukewarm* goes beyond emotional expression, however. The church is arrogant in an isolationist way, believing they need nothing from others. They cannot see how wretched and pitiable they are. As with many that Jesus counseled during his time on earth, they are blind to the reality of their situation. The message closes by saying, "Let anyone who has an ear listen to what the Spirit is saying to the churches" (3:22).

The challenge in reading the Bible, particularly with coded books like the Revelation, is in finding meaningful applications for our lives today. The message to the church at Laodicea is a warning against living half-heartedly or distractedly. Similar to

---

Similar to praying with one eye open, when we do not give ourselves fully to the present moment we squander the gift of being human.

---

praying with one eye open, when we do not give ourselves fully to the present moment we squander the gift of being human. We not only rob ourselves of the full-embodied experience, we rob those around us, too. Everything we do, down to the smallest detail, affects others. When we live half-heartedly, the experience others receive from us is equally half-hearted.

The message I receive from this passage in the Revelation is that passion is a gift intended for use, and we should apply it, appropriately, at every opportunity. Far from a mandate to fly off the handle half-cocked, it suggests we enter every moment with our entire being engaged – head, heart, body, and soul. One of the commandments Moses received from God on Mount Sinai (Deuteronomy 6:5) is this: "You shall love the Lord your God with all your heart, and with all your soul, and with all your strength." Should we not also *live* our moments with all our heart, soul, and strength? If anything is worth doing, it is worth doing with everything we have at our disposal, whether we are praying, working, resting, or playing.

In art, the color red brings a painted picture to life, just like the blood coursing through our veins, just like splashes of red transform a sunrise or sunset from mundane to spectacular. Our human passions inject zeal into our life on earth. We were not created to be lukewarm. It does no good to die with a reserve of passion any more than it does to limit how often we tell those closest to us how much we love them. The stores of loving energy are infinite, so we need not worry about depleting the supply.

Passion is a precious gift. Yes, it hurts when the object of our passion dies or fails or otherwise falls short of our hopes and dreams. Vulnerability necessarily accompanies giving our all to a person or goal. But what do we have to lose, really? The biggest loss is in *not* focusing ourselves fully on the situation before us because we cannot retrieve or relive our moments once they pass. The more we give, the more joy, beauty, and pleasure we stand to gain in return. It is not our place to judge whether what we can give is good enough, is better or worse than what others have to give, or that it makes the impact we feel it should. Our gifts are our gifts, and God intends us to heat them up or cool them down, but not allow them to become lukewarm.

Chapter 6

The Redeeming Face of Love

If I give away all my possessions, and if I hand over my body so that I may boast, but do not have love, I gain nothing.
1 Corinthians 13:3

The thirteenth chapter of Paul's first letter to the Corinthians is the *love chapter* of the Bible. It describes love as patient and kind, slow to anger, and not resentful. Love bears, believes, hopes, and endures all things. Love never fails. It sets an impossibly high standard for those of us who are merely human. As we experience it in close relationships, love displays many faces, some of which do not live up to Paul's description.

Indeed, love evolves through different phases. Perhaps the most elemental form of love is gravity – the mutual attraction between two bodies. Gravity holds us to the earth (even when we are upside down) and holds the earth and planets in their orbits around the sun. In the same way, loving relationships ground us. There is an inherent need in all of creation to be grounded in a relationship with another. Of course, love manifests in romance, but there is also the love between a parent and child, brotherly/sisterly love, platonic love, love of country, love of food or drink, love of deep conversations, love of guitars – the list is endless for the subjects and objects of our love. Each relationship is unique, attractive, and endearing in its own way.

The love of God for us, however, is unconditional. The Greek word for God's love is *agape* (ah-GAH-pay). While we talk a good game about loving someone unconditionally, human love is always conditional. The object of our love can only hurt or otherwise betray us so many times before the intensity of our love wanes. We may withdraw some

---

The absence of love leads people to all sorts of self-destructive behaviors – addictions, associations with abusers, and other unhealthy lifestyles.

---

of what we have given in love for our own protection, and sometimes for the good of the other. If the one to whom we offer love abuses us in dangerous ways, self-preservation requires our extraction. We often measure human love by time. A relationship that spans many years is a rare treasure, even though quantity does not always indicate quality. A special bond forms through the endurance of many trials, however.

A common trait to every type of love is the affirming nature of the love experience. It may only be a pet who greets us as if there were no one in the world they would rather see, but there is nothing like being loved in tangible ways to give us a sense of worth and purpose. The absence of love leads people to all sorts of self-destructive behaviors – addictions, associations with abusers, and other unhealthy lifestyles. When we do not feel loved, we question our value, our worthiness, and our reason for being. The absence of love leads to anger directed inward. I am told that infants who are not held and loved in their early days may die in spite of receiving adequate nourishment. Children and adolescents without stable, supportive, loving families often seek affirmation from gangs, drugs, or other less-than-desirable sources. Severe loneliness, particularly among the elderly, is an epidemic today.

When we have no loving relationships – when we feel unloved and uncared for or about – we find ourselves in a hell on earth. Without debating the notion of hell as an after-death destination of eternal punishment for unredeemed sinners, we can be certain that hell is a present reality of the here and now for many unloved people. Hell, in any of its theorized states, is a separation from the loving attention of others.

There is no substitute for a one-on-one, face-to-face, respectful and affirming relationship with another. For love to manifest in a reassuring, lasting manner, it must be embodied. Without love, nothing else matters, as Paul makes clear in his letter to the Corinthians. Withholding our loving attention from others hurts both them and us. They will seek love elsewhere, but what will we do – reserve our store of loving attention for someone more worthy? We seriously miss the point in doing so. Others *become* worthy by receiving our loving attention. That is the nature of God's agape love, which is the originating source of all manifestations of love. We *become* loved and loving by *allowing* God's love to permeate in and through us, even as it overflows onto others. It is through the giving and receiving of love that redemption spreads to all. It requires little – a card, a phone call, or a smile.

Chapter 7

The Sign of Jonah

Then some of the scribes and Pharisees said to him, "Teacher, we wish to see a sign from you." But he answered them, "An evil and adulterous generation asks for a sign, but no sign will be given to it except the sign of the prophet Jonah."
Matthew 12:38-39

Many of us were taught the story of the prophet Jonah as children in Sunday School. It is recorded in the short Old Testament book of his name. God told Jonah to go to the city of Nineveh to warn them of their impending destruction because of their wicked ways. Jonah hated the Ninevites and believed they deserved to die. Because he did not want them to have an opportunity to repent, he boarded a ship headed away from Nineveh. God caused a great storm that threatened to break the ship apart. The others on the ship were terrified and wondered who was responsible for this calamity. Jonah confessed that he had disobeyed his God, who was causing the storm to punish him. He told the sailors to throw him overboard, which they did, and the storm abated. Instead of drowning, however, a "large fish" [1] swallowed Jonah, where he remained for three days and three nights. Jonah repented in the belly of the fish, and God had the fish spew him out onto dry land. God, again, told Jonah to go to Nineveh to warn the people of their impending destruction. He went, provided the warning, the people heeded his words, turned from their evil ways, and "God changed his mind about the calamity that he had said he would bring upon them, and he did not do it."[2]

Jonah was angry with God as this was exactly what he feared would happen. In Jonah's mind, the destruction of the Ninevites was a right and just punishment. Instead, God showed mercy to this most undeserving of people. Jonah confessed his reason for trying to flee from God's command: "…for I knew

---

When God wants something done, it will be done whether we do it willingly or grudgingly.

---

that you are a gracious God and merciful, slow to anger, and abounding in steadfast love, and ready to relent from punishing."[3] Whether one reads the story of Jonah literally or allegorically, the lesson is the same: God's actions and purposes do not always fall in line with what we believe is best or just. God will be who God will be, unapologetically.

In the context of the story of Jonah, what does Jesus mean by saying "No sign will be given to (this

---

[1] Jonah 1:17
[2] Jonah 3:10
[3] Jonah 4:2

evil and adulterous generation) except the sign of the prophet Jonah"[4]? It is an interesting question with a number of possible answers. First, when God wants something done, it will be done whether we do it willingly or grudgingly. If we run in another direction, we may find ourselves swallowed by a metaphorical fish and spit up on the very ground where we were directed to go. Therefore, one sign of Jonah is that God's will *will* be done, with or without our enthusiastic participation.

Another telling sign of Jonah has to do with God's inexplicable grace. The people of Nineveh were not good people, at least not by the standards of the day. According to the story, and consistent with other biblical stories, God had every reason to destroy them. Like a benevolent guardian, however, God wanted to warn them of their impending demise and give them another opportunity to redeem themselves. Here is another sign of Jonah: God gives second and third chances, regardless of how we feel about it.

A third sign from the story of Jonah is God's love for us, even when we are unloving. Jonah fell into a significant sulk after the redemption of Nineveh. He was angry with God, but God understood and loved him, anyway.

Finally, Jesus says that only the evil ask for a sign, as if they need to see a miracle before they decide to change their ways. In the story of Jonah, however, God sent an unwilling prophet to give a reluctant message of repentance. For whatever reason, the people heard and heeded Jonah's words. Sometimes, even when we feel we need a divine sign, the Spirit

---

[4] Matthew 12:39

moves within us to nudge us in a direction closer to God.

Even though the Matthew passage seems to imply the sign of Jonah is one of judgment and punishment for sin, consistent with many passages from Matthew's telling, the final message is one of grace. Ultimately, the sign of Jonah is one of love and redemption, and that is the sign given by Jesus.

Chapter 8

The Exodus Revisited

Then the Lord said, "I have observed the misery of my people who are in Egypt; I have heard their cry on account of their taskmasters. Indeed, I know their sufferings, and I have come down to deliver them from the Egyptians, and to bring them up out of that land to a good and broad land, a land flowing with milk and honey." Exodus 3:7-8

This is the story of the exodus of the Israelites from Egypt. It is revisited in seemingly every telling of their history. Pharaoh made them slaves because he feared their growing numbers. Moses was sent to deliver them out of Egypt, but Pharaoh was uncooperative. God sent a series of plagues upon the people of Egypt until Pharaoh relented, agreeing to let the people go in return for ending the plagues. As they were making their way out of Egypt, however, Pharaoh changed his mind and sent his army after them. Trapped between the Red Sea and Pharaoh's army, God parted the waters of the sea to allow the Israelites safe passage through. Pharaoh's army followed and drowned when God released the waters back into the sea after the people arrived safely on the other shore. Once out of the grasp of Pharaoh, the people wandered in the wilderness for 40 years, waiting for their promised entry into the land known today as Israel.

We can read stories in the Bible literally – in this case as a historical reading – or we can seek for an allegorical understanding. I will follow the latter course for this reflection because I believe the story has much to tell us about ourselves, regardless of its historical accuracy. More specifically, I believe the story of the exodus is *our* story.

Those familiar with the story's details will recall that the Israelites' joy of being freed from their oppression in Egypt was short-lived. Life in the wilderness was hard. They expected to be released into the Promised Land quickly, but it took 40 years.

The story has much to tell us about ourselves regardless of its historical accuracy. The story of the exodus is **our** *story.*

In Biblical terminology, that is one generation, meaning the majority of those finally entering the Promised Land had little or no recollection of their years in slavery. More than once, the people felt that returning to bondage in Egypt would be better than wandering aimlessly in the wilderness, waiting on the timing of a God they feared had abandoned them.

There is a story written by St. John of the Cross, a 16th Century Spanish mystic, titled *The Dark Night of the Soul*. Its simplified premise is that those sincerely seeking union with God will come to a time when they can glimpse what an awakened life would be like, but they are not there, yet. In fact, they are trapped between their old life, to which they cannot return, and the new life they have yet to attain. They find themselves in a no-man's land that John of the Cross called the *Dark Night of the Soul.* There is no way out of the dark night except by going through it, trusting in God's timing and provision.

We all go through various *dark nights* in our lives, from getting through a difficult week of final exams to finishing an uncomfortable course of treatment for a medical condition. We can see the goal, but we are not there, yet. Dark nights may last for days, weeks, or years. For the Israelites, it lasted a generation.

Many of us, as we pass from the first to the second half of our lives, notice that much of what we worked so hard to attain in our earlier life loses its luster. The image of ourselves that we struggled to build now seems shallow, transitory, and insufficient. The stuff we so desired to accumulate becomes a burden. As we transition into our mature years, many of us long to be unbound from the binds we once so ardently sought. We can visualize a "Promised Land" out there, but we are not there, yet. Like the Israelites wandering through the wilderness, we grow restless and impatient with the current state of our lives, but we feel powerless to change it.

Who and what will we be when most of what we have treasured is left behind? As we age, we seek eternal treasures and shun the non-essentials of earth. Relationships grow in importance. The transition is difficult and can leave us adrift in a wilderness of our own creation. The story of the exodus assures us there is a Promised Land out there, and we will reach it one day – not on our timeline, however, but on God's.

Chapter 9

Bits and Bytes

Desire without knowledge is not good, and one who moves too hurriedly misses the way. Proverbs 19:2

I took a computer programming class in college in the 1970s. The lone computer at the university was the size of a small house with a fraction of the computing power of our mobile phones today. The computer read our instructions with *punch cards,* which required entering one precise instruction, i.e., "Start with 10," on a single card before going to the next precise order on a different card. Our final class project was to write a program so the computer would count down from 10 to 0 by ones. It required 80+ punch cards. The slightest mistake in punching or ordering the cards resulted in a failed project. It was tedious, mind-numbing, and unforgiving work.

Bits and *bytes* are the building blocks of computer language, then as now. A bit (binary digit) is a single data point, either 0 or 1. There are only two options for a bit – on or off. A byte is a grouping of 8 bits. In a computer's binary byte code, writing 0, 1, 2 looks like this: 00000000, 00000001, 00000010.

Prior to computers, we had pen and paper, typewriters, and slide rules with which to write and compute. Clearly, computers have provided giant leaps forward in making nearly every aspect of our lives easier and more efficient. In order for a computer to work, however, our information must be converted to a digital format – bits and bytes. Computers operate on a completely dualistic system – something must either be right or wrong, black or white, good or evil, on or off. There is no gray area in a digital language. A bit either has an electrical charge or it doesn't, and therein lies the problem. No matter how small the space between on and off, there is an *in between* with an infinite range of intermediate possibilities – possibilities where the spirit inhabits.

While I am far from suggesting a return to our pre-computer days, much has been lost in return for convenience and efficiency. I would term was has been lost as *depth* of experience. It wasn't that long ago that even an untrained eye could distinguish between a digitalized picture, i.e., a pictures taken on a cellphone (which converts the image into bits and bytes), and a picture taken with a good, film camera. The difference was in the depth of field, color, and contrast. Digital pictures were convenient, but not very representative. Now, with enough pixels (bits and bytes), the untrained human eye cannot tell the difference between a digital and a film picture in most cases. Yet, the difference is there in the spaces the bits and bytes cannot capture.

The situation is similar with sound recordings. The music we hear on the most prevalent sound sources today, reproduce only a small sample of the original sound. The result is usually difficult for the untrained ear to distinguish. The convenience makes it worthwhile for most of us, however, myself included.

Here is my concern in this discussion: Are we becoming blind to the depth of experience we lose for the convenience we gain? Far from suggesting a return to slide rules and typewriters, are there areas where we *can* distinguish the difference in depth such that the losses do not outweigh the gains? For example, having a digitalized church service available on line is a convenience for shut-ins, but the

---

Reading a book about love is not the same as actually experiencing a loving relationship.

---

experience is far less than being present in the sanctuary. Listening to a recording of a live musical performance makes the performance more accessible but is usually a poor substitute for actually being present for the performance. Reading a book about love is not the same as actually experiencing a loving relationship. Bits and bytes, like words and phrases, substitute for the depth of the actual experience. The field of Artificial Intelligence, exciting as it is, is still incapable of reading between the *on or off* options available to each bit upon which it depends.

When we text or email instead of speaking in person, we are essentially converting the spoken word into bits and bytes by losing all of the non-verbal context. In the same way, we sacrifice the depth of a hand-written note for the convenience of a text.

Again, my point is not that our new technologies

should be dropped for the old. Rather, it is that we need to be discerning about when and in what situations we use which method. To do otherwise is like praying with one eye open. Will we lose something of value by taking the easier, more convenient path? Our important relationships, like our spiritual development, cannot be captured in nor reduced to bits and bytes.

Good representation of dualistic thinking

Chapter 10

Silent Prayer

Likewise the Spirit helps us in our weakness; for we do not know how to pray as we ought, but that very Spirit intercedes with sighs too deep for words. Romans 8:26

Most of us learned to pray with words, by which I mean we spoke our prayers. Because language is how we were taught to communicate with each other, why would we not also communicate with God in the same way? It makes sense, and nothing I say after this point is intended to belittle or discourage the saying of spoken prayers. There are other types of prayer, however, that one may find comforting and effective, depending on the need. Silent prayer is one such type of prayer for me.

I have heard various estimates of how much of our communication with each other is actually transmitted by the words we use. A common estimate is about 10%, meaning approximately 90% of the communication received is non-verbal – body language, tone of voice, facial expression, attentiveness, etc. If I tell you that I love you while I am looking at my cell phone, what message do you receive? Certainly not one of love or devotion. The words lose their literal meaning because my non-verbal behavior is inconsistent with what comes out of my mouth. Could the same be true with God – that the words we use in prayer falter when our attitude and body language are not consistent with our words?

I receive regular reminders that I should speak less and listen more (for good reason, no doubt). When I interrupt or say something flippant in an attempt to lighten the mood or redirect a conversation, I send the message that I am not engaged with what is being said. Regardless of whether that is my conscious intent, regardless of what words I use, regardless of my body language,

> *Perhaps God has a message for us – one we cannot receive until we stop talking and listen.*

that is the message that will be received. The point is that what we communicate and the words we use are often very different, whether we are talking to a friend, a significant other, or God.

While God, no doubt, is interested in what we have to say, I believe God already knows. The Bible tells us that God knows what is in and on our hearts, probably better than we know. Certainly, one of the benefits of spoken prayer is simply the exercise of putting what is on our minds into words – not for God's sake, but for ours. Sometimes the very act of putting feelings into words helps define what is

How do I know what I think until I hear myself say it?

troubling us and may even suggest a course of action. On the other hand, perhaps God has a message for us -- one we cannot receive until we stop talking and listen. Thus, the importance, at least for some of us, of incorporating silent prayer into our prayer practice.

In my experience, listening for a message from God is different than hearing a message from a friend. I, personally, have never heard God speak in words or with a human-like voice. Opening our ears to God is more like assuming a responsive stance that opens us to God's guidance. Again, in my experience, an occasional short period of waiting to hear from God is not likely to produce anything useful, nor do messages from God necessarily come at the time we seek them. It is not that God is not willing to communicate with us. The problem is that our distractedness prevents us from being able to receive God's communications. I find God's messages arriving as inspirations while I am going about my daily activities. Sometimes God speaks through an inspired thought that enters my head, sometimes it's an inspired meaning from a scripture passage, sometimes it's in something I read or hear from a friend. I believe a regular assumption of a silent, receptive posture for extended periods – 20 minutes at a time, once or twice a day – helps orient something within us toward receiving an occasional divine message.

Sitting in the presence of God in silence is more of a *communion* than a conversation. Saying a prayer with words is *doing* prayer; silent prayer is *being* prayer. Both are useful and important. To use only one method is like praying with one eye open. The technique of silent prayer native to Christianity, dating back many centuries, is called *Centering Prayer*. Appendix A in the back of this book contains an *Intro to Centering Prayer*.

Because God is non-verbal for most of us, finding non-verbal ways to commune with God are essential in establishing a two-way relationship where we seek to listen and not simply to be heard.

Chapter 11

Praying Together

Pray then in this way... Matthew 6:9a

Earlier in 2019 I spent several days with a group of Benedictine monks south of Boston. I was allowed to join them during parts of their daily schedule, including the five daily worship services. One part of most worship services was what they consider *praying together*, which in this case was chanting the Psalms. They sat in two groups facing each other and chanted passages from the Psalms, sometimes one side at a time, other times in unison.

For the most part, I was taught that prayer was a solitary activity – me and God. Certainly, there were prayers before meals and bedtime where one person would pray on behalf of those present at the table or bedside. In church, the pastor would pray on behalf of the entire congregation. Those were community prayers, but it was still one person doing the praying while the others sat in silence. The exception was *The Lord's Prayer*, which was recited in unison as a community. With those exceptions, I considered prayer a solitary activity.

It is interesting that the prayer Jesus instructed his disciples to pray was a community prayer. The language is distinctly communal:
Our Father;
Give *us* this day *our* daily bread;
Forgive *us our* trespasses as *we* forgive those who trespass against *us;*
Lead *us* not into temptation;
Deliver *us* from evil.
I have tried praying this prayer in an individual way, i.e., *My* Father; give *me* this day, etc., but it feels wrong and selfish. Perhaps that is because I learned it as a communal prayer; or perhaps the prayer loses its power when removed from its communal context. It is also interesting that three verses before giving his disciples The Lord's Prayer, Jesus says, "But whenever you pray, go into your room and shut the door and pray to your Father who is in secret" (Matthew 6:6). The latter prayer process is a distinctly solitary activity.

I suspect Jesus' message is that *both* individual and community prayers are important. Nor should this surprise anyone. The community aspect of prayer, however, is the one I find most challenging. Actually, it is my ego that finds community prayer most challenging. My ego-self desires a special relationship with God – one that sets me apart from others as a unique creation in God's eyes. And there is biblical evidence for that very uniqueness (see Psalm 139). What trips me up is that *everyone* is a unique creation of God, loved and known for their individual traits by our doting, divine Parent. Wouldn't that make any individual, i.e., *me,* less special? Although my ego is bruised at the thought, I believe we are *all* precious beyond belief in God's eyes.

In his prayer in the Garden of Gethsemane on the night before his crucifixion (John 17), Jesus prays that we, as in *all* of us, might be one with him just as he is one with God. There is an unmistakable communal inclusiveness to his words. In Paul's letters, he describes us as the body of Christ (see Romans 12), identifying individuals as various parts of the one body. Again, this is not welcome news to the ego self who is more than willing to forego the salvation of many others in order to assure salvation for itself and those it deems worthy.

As I age and the more I read, the more convinced I become that salvation is communal. In other words, we become one with God together – as one body – or we do not become one with God at all, except perhaps in brief awakenings. This is why

---

As we awaken to our oneness, we understand that we cannot be well until all others are well, too.

---

healing the sick, easing suffering, feeding the hungry, and including the outcast – the hallmarks of Jesus' ministry – are so vitally important for us to focus on today. As we awaken to our oneness, we understand that we cannot be well until all others are well. And so praying together should be an important part of our prayer practice. It is an affirmation of our unity.

Personally, I recite the Lord's Prayer as a regular part of my daily devotions. When I do, however, I try to assume the posture of being one part of a large body praying for and with the entire community of my brothers and sisters. No doubt, there are countless others across the globe and through the ages praying it with me.

Jesus gave us a new commandment, to love one another. Praying together is one way for us to fulfil that commandment.

Chapter 12

Walking Prayer

Ever since the creation of the world his eternal power and divine nature, invisible though they are, have been understood and seen through the things he has made. Romans 1:20

I have heard and believe that the original Bible is creation itself. In other words, for those desiring a knowledge of God in the days before written scrolls and before most people were able to read any scrolls they had access to, people could learn everything they needed to know about God from nature, as we can still today. To me, it makes perfect sense. If all of creation springs from God, all of creation must be imbued with God's nature. In other words, I believe God is *in* all of creation, and so by absorbing an in-depth knowledge of the essence of any created thing, we find the imprint of God. Believing that God is *in* everything is called *panentheism,* as opposed to the belief that everything *is* God, which is *pantheism.*

To believe that God is in everything means, to me, that God experiences *through* us. As we go through life's sorrows and joys, God rides the waves of our emotional ups and downs with us. God weeps as we weep, hurts as we hurt, laughs as we laugh, and loves as we love. When we say that we are God's feet and hands, we mean that God *literally* works through us – serving the needy, healing the sick, welcoming the outcast. Of course, God also grants us free will, so we must cooperate in order for God to work in and through us.

The following prayer, written by St. Teresa of Avila, expresses the panentheistic nature of God well:

Christ has no body now but yours.
No hands, no feet on earth but yours.
Yours are the eyes through which
He looks compassion on this world,
Yours are the feet with which He walks to do good,
Yours are the hands through which he blesses all the world.
Yours are the hands, yours are the feet,
Yours are the eyes, you are His body.
Christ has no body now on earth but yours.[5]

One of the many ways we can connect with God in nature, as well as allowing God to experience nature through us, is through walking prayer, also called meditative or mindful walking. It involves walking in an unhurried, deliberate manner, focusing on the various details our senses take in. We stop to gaze at the amazing intricacy of a single leaf or the veins of a pebble, we breathe the intoxicating fragrance of the honeysuckle, listen to the soulful coo of the mourning dove, or taste the sweet nectar of a buttercup. We take our time and focus our attention

---

[5] https://www.goodreads.com/quotes/66880-christ-has-no-body-now-but-yours-no-hands-no

on the amazing particularities of the world around us, one small detail at a time.

We focus particularly on what is rising into our body from the earth through our feet. We feel the firm, dependable support of the earth beneath us. More than that, however, we feel the spirit, the energy rising from the earth – the earth from which our bodies were formed and to which they will return. There is a constant flow of loving energy between us and the earth that we completely miss as we hurry about our days. The gravity that holds us to the earth

---

There is a constant flow of loving energy between us and the earth that we completely miss as we hurry about our days.

---

is loving energy cradling us to itself, as is the gravitational field keeping the earth in its orbit around the sun, and the force holding atomic particles in their infinitesimal structures – all divine love in action: attracting, giving, and receiving. We recognize ourselves as one station in the infinite flow of love energy, permeating the unique creation we are, and sent off again into the universe with a blessing only we can give. As we mindfully move in walking prayer, we sense our part in this flow of the life in which we live and move and have our being. Walking barefoot, where it can safely be done, is optimal.. Even seated, with bare feet in the grass, can connect us with the earth in wonderful, moving ways.

Getting in touch with God in nature through walking prayer is one way to focus our awareness on

God's constant presence with and within us. Once we are aware, and once we consent to God's promptings within, we become available as instruments of good for God's will and work on earth, as St. Teresa reminds us is our calling. Walking prayer is one way for us to be Christ to God's creation, while allowing God's creation to be Christ to us.

A guide to meditative walking is included in Appendix B at the end of this book.

Chapter 13

Fear and Awe

The angel said to her, "Do not be afraid, Mary, for you have found favor with God." Luke 1:30

Fear may be our biggest barrier to a happier, more fulfilled life. True, the Bible tells us that the *fear* of God is the beginning of knowledge,[6] and that we are to *fear* our God.[7] Fear, however, may also be our biggest barrier to a closer relationship with God. The type of fear referred to in these passages, however, is better described as *awe* than by what we consider fear today. Awe is the feeling of looking out over the edge of the Grand Canyon or gazing into a clear night sky without the interference of city lights. Awe is the feeling when a newborn wraps her tiny fingers around yours. Awe is our response when experiencing something breathtakingly beautiful, yet completely beyond words. When we are gifted with such an experience, when we are touched by such grace, our natural tendency to try to understand or explain falls

---

[6] Proverbs 1:7
[7] Leviticus 19:14

away and leaves us stilled in not knowing and, somehow, not needing to know.

There are numerous biblical references encouraging us to *fear* God and many more telling us not to be *afraid*. As we learn to distinguish between fear and awe, we understand this is not a contradiction. God is so far beyond our comprehension that the only reasonable reaction to pondering God is *awe*. Fear, on the other hand, results from a lack of faith – a lack of faith in the inherent goodness of ourselves and others, a lack of faith that we are loved and cared for, and a lack of faith that God will make

---

Fear may be our biggest barrier to a happier, more fulfilled life.

---

all things work together for good.[8] That sort of fear stands as a barrier between us as we are today and the person God encourages us to become. We can begin to overcome our faithless fears by developing a more intimate relationship with God through scripture, in nature, or through others.

One helpful way to read and understand the Bible is as a personal message from God. Granted, this requires more than a cursory reading. In fact, it often involves reading a particular passage many times, slowly, and out loud. It is helpful to read a commentary about each passage, researching the context and culture from which the passage arose. What did it mean when it was written? How does it

---

[8] Romans 8:28

translate to the world today? What is God saying to *me* in this story or passage? Where do I fit into the story? Engaging the Bible in this manner is a way of praying the scripture – entering the message in an intimate and open way. Fear springs from a lack of knowledge. Once we better understand what underlies our fear, our sense of helplessness eases. As we come to know more about the nature of God, our fear gives way to awe.

Placing ourselves into scripture is a key. The Old Testament stories of the Israelites' road to freedom is our story – from what form of bondage are we trying to escape? How does their struggle mirror ours? In the story of the Good Samaritan,[9] are we the beaten person left by the side of the road? Are we among the religious folks who pass him by? Are we the one who stops to help? Chances are we have played each of these roles at different times in our lives. What if God's message to Mary in Luke 1:30 is God's message to us: "Do not be afraid, (insert your name here), for *you* have found favor with God." When we place ourselves into the stories of the Bible, scripture comes alive for us.

The Latin term for reading the scripture in this manner is *Lectio Divina*, or sacred reading. It is a formal method of praying the scriptures, or placing ourselves into scripture. Perhaps finding ourselves in scripture is more accurate. It is one way for God to speak directly to us through a sacred text. God has spoken through scripture to hundreds of generations before us, and will continue to do so for countless generations to come. A copy of an *Introduction to Lectio*

---

[9] Luke 10:25-37

Divina is included in Appendix C at the end of this book.

Our search for a happier, more fulfilled life necessarily creates a desire to know God more. While we are incapable of knowing God in all of God's fullness, by praying the scriptures we can assure ourselves that God will not desert us. God's love, presence, and care through all of life's challenges is dependable. Life is not always easy or pleasant, but praying the scriptures helps us live in God's presence with more awe and less fear.

Chapter 14

Praying the Details

Then Jesus told them a parable about their need to pray always and not lose heart. Luke 18:1

I tend to think of God as a big-picture being. By this I mean to say that God is unfathomably expansive, inclusive, and larger-than-life. Such a God would not get bogged down in the minutia of our lives. If God is keeping planets in their orbits, there is certainly no time to attend to my latest facial blemish or the mixed message I may have received from an acquaintance the other day. Like many of us, I grew up believing that God was big and I was small. Praying for a good grade on a test I had not prepared adequately for was much too trivial an issue to trouble God about.

As I grow older, I continue to believe God is focused on the big picture. I also believe, however, that God is focused on the minutia. If God truly lives in and acts through us, and since the small details of our lives demand a large portion of our attention and resources, then it stands to reason that God attends to every small detail along with us. My teacher and mentor, Fr. Richard Rohr, says that God loves things by becoming them. To the extent that is true, the more we know and understand something *in its richest detail*, the more we can know and understand about God. Not that everything around us *is* God, but that God exists in the details of everything around us.

We see this playing out in our relationships with others. We cannot really know a person until we know details about their life and being. Ironically, the more we know about someone, the more difficult it becomes to describe them accurately to others. It is easy to dismiss a homeless person on the street when we keep our distance from him or her. It is much more difficult to ignore their plight when we take a few minutes to visit with them, listen to their story, see the color of their eyes, and learn other details of

> **If God truly lives in and acts through us, it stands to reason that God attends to every small detail along with us.**

their existence. If we dare to look in their eyes, we may experience a soulful tug that changes something inside of us, making it impossible to continue to see this person as an anonymous member of a homogeneous group outside of our circle of interest. Details matter. We also experience this in race relations. It is too easy to glance at those of other ethnic backgrounds and believe they all look and act alike, lumping them into a single, usually negative racial stereotype. And of course we will not be able to distinguish the unique character of any particular individual until we learn something about their details. We will not see God in them until we look in their eyes and take a genuine interest in who they are beyond their outer appearance.

In praying for others, the details matter. When someone asks for me to pray for them or for someone else, I ask for as many details as they are comfortable sharing with me. On the one hand, I want to respect their privacy. On the other hand, I want to be able to visualize where the pain is so my prayer can be focused there. Knowing the details helps in that process.

In the same way, details matter in my personal prayers. It is not that God is not already aware of every little aspect of my issues, but that my awareness is likely deficient. There are almost certainly parts of the issue that I deny, repress, or otherwise prefer not to acknowledge. There may be connections to my past that I have completely ignored. I am probably reacting in ways that are consistent with the ways I have always reacted to difficult situations, and those reactions may not be helpful or honest. Being up front with God about the entire situation, searching for and sorting through the details with God is helpful once we know God as non-judgmental and accepting of us as and where we are.

Revealing the details of our situation to God and others is uncomfortable because it makes us vulnerable. Making ourselves vulnerable – revealing ourselves in our essential nakedness – allows God to meet us in our pain, which is where healing begins. Praying vague, generic prayers is like praying with one eye open in that we are not fully giving ourselves over in prayer. Praying the details is surrendering ourselves to God where those details can be resurrected into something better.

Chapter 15

The Second Arrow

A soft answer turns away wrath, but a harsh word stirs up anger. The tongue of the wise dispenses knowledge, but the mouths of fools pour out folly. Proverbs 15:1-2

All human beings possess a secret wisdom-power. It is not secret because it is hidden but because it is so seldom used. It is the power to pause and reflect prior to reacting. Taking a short pause before responding to a situation almost always has a positive impact on what happens in the aftermath. As a hypothetical example, I have a strained relationship with a co-worker who angrily barges into my office and accuses me of starting a nasty rumor about her personal life. I vehemently deny starting the rumor and immediately accuse her of being the source of the rumor since all she ever talks about is her personal life. Using the metaphor of arrows, the first arrow, in this case, was my co-worker angrily barging into my office and falsely accusing me. It probably hurt. The second arrow, however, was my angry reaction, which wounded her right back. Which arrow is most likely to perpetuate the strained relationship? The second arrow, of course. Because I responded on gut instinct instead of using my super-power to pause and reflect before reacting, I loosed a second arrow that made a stressful situation worse. We can blame the first arrow for initiating the ugly process, but we cannot grow spiritually until we recognize and accept responsibility for the second arrow.

In Buddhism there is the lesson of *The Second Arrow*, which goes like this:

> "The Buddha was giving a teaching to an assembly of his monks and nuns. He asked, "If a person is struck by an arrow, is it painful?"
>
> The monks and nuns replied, "Yes, it is."
>
> The Buddha then asked, "If the person is struck by a second arrow, is that even more painful?"
>
> The assembly replied again, "Yes, it is."
>
> Then the Buddha explained, "In life, we cannot always control the first arrow. However, the second arrow is our reaction to the first. The second arrow is optional."
>
> As long as we are alive, we will have painful experiences, which are like the first arrow. To get all upset by the first arrow and condemn, judge, criticize, hate, or deny the first arrow is like being struck by a second arrow. Many times the first arrow is out of our control, but the arrow of reactivity is not."[10]

---

[10] Jerome Freedman, *The Second Arrow.* http://mountainsangha.org/second-arrow/, January 3, 2015.

My workplace example, above, is about a relationship with a co-worker. Had I considered how best to react, I might have been able to redeem the first arrow into an opportunity for healing the brokenness between us. I might have invited a deeper exploration of her pain and fear. Who knows, I might have even discovered something in myself that was subtlety contributing to the situation. There is an old saying, attributed as Native American wisdom, that goes, "I will not criticize a person until I have walked 30 days in her shoes." Everyone is fighting a difficult battle of which we know little.

The lesson of *the Second Arrow,* however, goes beyond interpersonal relationships to our own inner life. How we react to situations in our lives matters – not just because of its impact on others, but because of its impact on *us!* We cannot control who wages

How we react to situations in our lives matters – not just because of its impact on others, but because of its impact on us!

unfair criticism our way. We cannot control receiving a cancer diagnosis or being hit by a drunk driver or finding ourselves in the path of a tornado. We can, however, *always* control our response – the second arrow.

The difference between the first and second arrows mirrors the difference between pain and suffering. Pain happens to all of us – physical, emotional, and mental pain. It all hurts, but it is also a shared human experience. We are all pierced by the first arrow from time to time, so there is really no need to describe how much worse my pain is than yours. What we do with our pain, how we respond to our pain, determines the degree to which we suffer from that pain. This is a difficult lesson to learn because we all want to get rid of our pain, and rightly so. When we cannot change it, however, we need to find ways to live with it in the best way possible. That is how we minimize our suffering – by accepting that which we cannot change in this moment. That is how we keep our second arrow in its quiver where it will not deepen the wound already inflicted. That is using our super-power to pause and reflect before reacting.

Chapter 16

Dealing With Dharma

In the day of prosperity be joyful, and in the day of adversity consider; God has made the one as well as the other, so that mortals may not find out anything that will come after them.
Ecclesiastes 7:14

The literal meaning of the Sanskrit word, *dharma* (dar'-mah), is "the law." It does not mean the law in a dogmatic sense, however. We can break human laws. We can run from the upholders of the law. Through legislation, we can change the law. Dharma refers to a law that we cannot break, run from, or change. Dharma is the law of the moment. It refers to what is, right now. I can choose to be happy, sad, angry, or any of the infinite range of human emotions over the way things are in this moment, but it will not change the dharma – it will not change the situation of the moment. The only control I have over dharma is my response to it.

When we talk about living in the moment, we refer to a state of mind where we are not reliving past experiences, nor are we looking ahead with worry or anticipation over something that may or may not occur in the future. Living in the moment is about being fully present to whatever is occurring in my life *right now*. Indeed, the current moment is the only one we can actually experience, even though our attention is usually elsewhere. Remaining in the moment is a perpetual challenge, particularly in the West where our distractions are many.

Dharma is a familiar term in Buddhism and Hinduism. The concept of dharma is not foreign to Christianity, either, but over the past few centuries we have tended to look past it. We (mistakenly) believe ourselves less "victimized" by dharma since we have developed ways to better shelter ourselves from the extremes of the climate and make our lives more comfortable. As more of us have made ourselves safer and more secure from certain of life's disasters,

---

Changing the moment is beyond our control.
Changing our response to the moment,
however, is completely under our control.

---

we have convinced ourselves that there is little that we cannot avoid experiencing, even and especially the present moment. Floods, tornados, hurricanes, forest fires, theft, tsunamis and the like prove differently. We cannot shield ourselves from broken hearts, the loss of loved ones, or the steady decay of our bodies. Our ability to shelter ourselves from some things leads us to believe we can avoid all unpleasantness. Dharma says differently.

In order to deal successfully with dharma we must focus ourselves on the current moment, without dragging any baggage from the past or future. The way things are in this moment is the way things are in this moment, and nothing we do will change that. Changing the moment is beyond our control. Changing our response to the moment, however, is completely under our control, as is making changes in our lives that may help align future moments better with our desires. We are, at best, *co*-creators of our future moments. That is how we deal with dharma. It is expressed well in the Serenity Prayer:

God grant me the serenity to accept the things I cannot change,
The courage to change what I can, and the wisdom to know the difference.

The author of the Old Testament wisdom book of Ecclesiastes also speaks of the dharma by encouraging us to consider that God makes both good days and challenging days, the purpose of which is to keep us from knowing what comes next. As we learn to accept each day and each moment as it presents itself to us and still be thankful, it matters little what comes next. We know there are always blessings and challenges in every moment and getting upset about what is only makes the difficult times that much more difficult. Challenges, like blessings, pass.

Dealing with the dharma is about harmonizing ourselves with reality. It does not mean we accept sub-standard or undesirable conditions, however. It does not mean we cease seeking to better the lives of ourselves and others. It only means we strive to enter each moment deeply and fully, without adding to or subtracting from it. Each moment is sufficient in and of itself. It is about maintaining a sense of equanimity through life's ups and downs. Every moment passes, for better or for worse. It requires trust that what is is from God, and the knowledge that if it is from God, it will eventually work together for good. In order to deal with dharma, we must accept – perhaps even enjoy – what we experience moment to moment.

Chapter 17

A Den of Thieves

Then Jesus entered the temple and drove out all who were selling and buying in the temple, and he overturned the tables of the money changers and the seats of those who sold doves. He said to them, "It is written, 'My house shall be called a house of prayer; but you are making it a den of robbers.'"
Matthew 21:12-13

There are few examples recorded in the Gospels of Jesus getting angry. We develop a picture of him as mostly even-tempered. He displayed displeasure at people who were misleading others, under the guise of religion, about what was required for salvation. He was seemingly frustrated by how slow his disciples were to grasp his message at times. But the top prize for flying off the handle goes to what we refer to as Jesus' "cleansing of the temple." In the various Gospel accounts, he overturns tables and chairs, runs off the sacrificial animals, and, quoting from Isaiah, says they have transformed God's house of prayer into a den of robbers. In John's account of the event,[11]

---

[11] John 2:13-16.

Jesus even weaves together a whip of cords to aid in the cleansing.

For the leaders of the temple, the business folks, and probably even for the people there to worship, Jesus' actions were those of a crazed lunatic. The buying and selling of sacrifices and the changing of money was a normal part of the temple experience. Seemingly, no one but Jesus saw anything wrong with it. And that is exactly the trap we can find ourselves in even today – that we become comfortable with and accept without question the possible turning of our temples into dens of thieves. It becomes so commonplace, we don't even notice until someone comes in, loses his or her temper, and starts throwing tables and chairs.

The concept of what constitutes a temple is worth reflecting upon. In Jesus' day, the temple was in Jerusalem and was the center of the Jewish faith. Its innermost part, the Holy of Holies, was the residence of God. No one was allowed entry to the Inner Sanctum except the High Priest, and then only once a year. Today, we often consider the buildings in which we worship – our churches, synagogues, mosques, and other buildings – as temples. But the Bible goes much further, naming our bodies as temples of the Most High. For example, in his first letter to the church at Corinth, Paul writes, "Do you not know that you are God's temple and that God's Spirit dwells in you?"[12] The temple that Jesus "cleansed" can be seen as a metaphor for us. In what ways have we turned our personal "house of prayer"

---

[12] 1 Corinthians 3:16.

into a "den of thieves?" In what ways have we blocked the path to our own Inner Sanctum?

Perhaps what Jesus railed against in the temple was the outrageous prices being charged and not just that commerce was being conducted. After all, his accusation was that the sellers were "robbers." The people were a captive audience in the temple, similar to us in airports today. We pay higher prices because it is more convenient than leaving the area to pay a more reasonable price. Deeper than that, however, one of Jesus' primary teachings was that the entire sacrificial system – that something else must die to cleanse us of our sins, or that we can buy our salvation – was a sham. God's love and forgiveness is given freely, and all we must do is receive it. Not only

> *One of Jesus' primary teachings was that the entire sacrificial system – that something else must die to cleanse us of our sins, or that we can buy our salvation – was a sham.*

do we not *need* to earn or pay for it, *we cannot earn or pay for it.* God's love is a gift. In that sense, the buyers and sellers were simply expensive and unnecessary distractions from the real point of being in the temple – to be in God's presence. There should be no cover charge for entry. Everything else simply draws our attention away from the primary purpose. And the leaders of the temple, then and now, smiled because the distractions often accrued to their benefit.

Even so, what about our personal temple? What obstacles prevent our bodies from being houses of prayer? Where are our distractions? Where are we wasting resources and energy to try to earn the gift God freely gives to us? What would Jesus throw out of our temple if he were to enter? Perhaps when we place conditions on the giving of our love and acceptance to others – the very love and acceptance lavished so freely on us – we become more of a den of thieves than a house of prayer. Loving attention is always life-giving and should always be free, whether given or received. Love is not a product for the marketplace.

Chapter 18

Difficult Decisions

I know your works; you are neither cold nor hot. I wish that you were either cold or hot. So, because you are lukewarm, and neither cold nor hot, I am about to spit you out of my mouth.
Revelation 3:15-16

I learned the most useful life lessons from a professor in graduate school who was effective because of *how* he taught, not because of *what* he taught. His teaching method was the same, regardless of the topic. His classes met once a week, and he assigned a number of journal articles about a specific issue for every class. Two hours prior to each class, students had to submit a paper describing the issue of the week, taking a position on the issue, and defending their position. The first hour of class was spent with the professor standing in front of the students, one at a time, announcing that student's position and initiating a class debate over that decision. While this professor was my most effective instructor, he was also the most uncomfortable and challenging. His classes were difficult because we knew that regardless of the position we chose, there would be strong arguments on the other side of the issue. This professor did not care what position we took as much as that our position was reflective of the assigned readings and that our position was definitive and defensible. If a student had not taken the time to carefully consider the options and reason through his or her decision, the professor would quickly expose the lack of preparation to the class.

The difficult decisions we make in life are hard because there are good arguments for more than one option. If there were only one good option, the decision would not be difficult. We have to choose based on the information we have at the time, accepting that our decision may prove less than optimal from a retrospective view in the future. Difficult decisions are a part of every life for several reasons. First, we cannot make a difference in life by

> *The difficult decisions we make in life are hard because there are strong arguments for more than one option.*

riding the fence on important issues. Life gains richness by exploring diverse options and new paths, so we miss much by attempting to live in a small, safe, non-confrontational world. Second, we cannot fully enter a decision by also keeping other options open. Like praying with one eye open, we cannot fully give ourselves to God or anyone or anything else by being tepid when it's time to make a choice. Finally, we learn to trust in God's goodness by making bad choices and failing, much more than we learn from good decisions and successes. The latter simply reaffirm our belief in our self-sufficiency. We learn that God works with us *regardless* of the choices we make, co-creating something good from the mess we often make of our lives.

Those of us in the United Methodist Church (UMC) face a difficult decision. The governing body recently affirmed and strengthened its position on the less-than-full inclusion of the LGBTQ community. It will almost certainly split the denomination, its churches, and family and friends within those churches. Individual congregations, and more importantly, individual members, have a difficult decision to make – remain a part of the UMC as it is currently constituted, or leave and go elsewhere. There are biblical arguments for the position adopted by the UMC, and there are biblical arguments against it. There are good, faithful people who support the position, and there are good, faithful people who do not support it. I believe UMC members, myself included, find themselves at an uncomfortable crossroads and must choose a path, recognizing that at some point, even doing nothing is a choice.

The question is *not* what the UMC did or will do. It is not even what my particular church family will decide. The key question is this: What will *I* decide and why? Can I defend my position in a well-reasoned, informed manner? This is a spiritual test, and we will be measured not so much for the choices we make, but for the methods by which we make our decisions. Did we defer to others? How did we prioritize the issues? Who benefits from this decision? Who does it exclude? Difficult decisions call for courage, regardless of the issue. This is not a time to rush to judgment, nor is it a time to be paralyzed into inaction.

My understanding of the message in Revelation to the church at Laodicea, quoted above, is to take a stand, hot or cold, right or wrong. It is time to weigh the options, make a choice, and trust God for what follows.

Chapter 19

A Beautiful Soul, Part 1

*I praise you, for I am fearfully and wonderfully made.
Wonderful are your works, that I know very well.*
Psalm 139:14

In 1970, singer/songwriter Don McLean wrote what would become the mega-hit song, *Vincent*. Millions of people, myself included, were obsessed with this poetic story set to music about the 19th Century artist, Vincent Van Gogh. The song is better known by its opening words, drawn from the title of one of Van Gogh's many paintings, *Starry, Starry Night*. The lyrics of the song blend the tragic life of this troubled artist with references to many of his works. After struggling with mental illness and poverty, Van Gogh committed suicide at age 37. The line from the song that haunted me then and now is this:

> *"And when no hope was left inside on that starry, starry night, you took your life as lovers often do;
> But I could've told you, Vincent, this world was never meant for one as beautiful as you."*[13]

In the mid-1970s and 80s, I was a folk-singer playing at bars and coffee houses, and *Vincent* was one of the most requested songs in my repertoire. Many people had the lyrics memorized and would solemnly sing along. I believe there is a powerful truth lying beneath these words that many of us relate to in a very personal way. That powerful something is impossible to fully express in words, but it can be triggered by words set to music, as McLean demonstrated. Once triggered, we know the

> ***What was perhaps clear to Van Gogh, but becomes clouded over in the daily grind of our lives is that at our essence, we are a pure and beautiful soul.***

experience in an unmistakable way. It has to do with the fact that each of us, like Van Gogh, has a soul that is too beautiful for this world. Many of us, in our most intimate and vulnerable moments, feel as though no one understands us. We feel mistreated, unappreciated, and alone – just as Van Gogh felt. When the people and circumstances in our world run roughshod over our tender essence, we feel we no longer belong. And we are right – that part of us is not of this world.

What was perhaps clear to Van Gogh, but becomes clouded over in the daily grind of our lives is

---

[13] Don McLean, *Vincent*. Universal Music Publishing Group, 1970.

that at our essence, we are a pure and beautiful soul. This applies to all of us, regardless of how inartistic we may believe ourselves to be. We enter this world as a fully developed soul in a minimally developed physical body. When our physical needs are satisfied, we are a wide-eyed sponge taking in the wonder and beauty of this mysterious, enticing, physical existence. It does not take long, however, to learn that this world, beautiful as it is, does not always reciprocate the love and wonder we attempt to bestow upon it. As we grow and mature, our physical being overshadows our spiritual nature in ways that can make our beautiful soul seem almost non-existent. We are protective of our precious essence, often unconsciously, because we know it is not of this world. Unfortunately, we become so protective as to almost shield it into obscurity. When we believe our beautiful soul may be wounded by this world, we double-down on our efforts to protect it. The abuse of drugs, alcohol, and other overly risky behaviors are often attempts at self-protection that dull the pain the world can inflict on our soft underbelly. Suicide is a tragic and far too common result of this inherently protective instinct.

Clearly, a balance between protection and expression is needed. By opening our beautiful soul to the world, all manner of awe-inspiring works are birthed, as witnessed by Van Gogh's paintings, McLean's song, well-prepared meals, and all the amazing works of life and art we enjoy. It is only when a person exposes his or her spiritual essence that an expression of the ethereal, unearthly beauty of the spiritual realm can be made manifest for us to see, feel, touch, taste, and smell. Unfortunately, the opening required for the soul leaves the person vulnerable. Part of the pain is the responsibility of those witnessing the soulful expression of another for not recognizing and appreciating the exposure required. Part of the responsibility rests upon the artist, too, in recognizing and accepting that a part of us really is too beautiful for this world. Finding effective strategies to cope with the tension is vital.

Repressing the expression of our beautiful souls is like praying with one eye open. We cannot become fully alive to our true nature without giving birth to physical expressions of our beautiful souls.

Chapter 20

A Beautiful Soul, Part 2

Then Jesus said, "Father forgive them; for they do not know what they are doing." Luke 23:34

There is a part of us that is truly too beautiful to be appreciated by or safe in the material world. Only when we are connected deep-unto-deep with others, soul to soul, can our most vulnerable centers express safely. Our physical existence, though beautiful and enticing, becomes cold, cruel, and manipulative when it represses its spiritual essence. Our spiritual nature desires to manifest in physical ways, whether in works of art, dance, food, children, or stimulating conversation. Truly beautiful and timeless works and performances come from a place deep within the artist that connect with a similar place deep within the audience. As long as we are physically embodied, our souls long to connect with other souls in meaningful, physical ways.

Part of our inner struggle results from our eternal souls residing in mortal bodies. The soul was never born and will never die. Our physical nature clings to that which the spirit creates, not wanting it to change and grow, knowing that growth eventually leads to decay and death. Our souls let go of embodied creation easily and gracefully, understanding that the natural life-cycle for every embodied thing is growth, decay, death, and rebirth. The soul knows that this process allows the earth and everything on it to be reborn as a new creation, increasing diversity, and expressing the fathomless creativity of the Divine.

Our individual souls are conduits for God's Spirit. They are our connection to God, and through that connection, where we are interwoven with everything else in creation, including with each other. An embodied soul can be (imperfectly) thought of as

---

Our physical nature clings to that which the spirit creates, not wanting it to change and grow, knowing that growth eventually leads to decay and death.

---

a clothed body. We put on clothes to protect our bodies from the environment, to fit in with those around us, and to prevent ourselves from being seen naked. Small children have no such inhibitions. As we grow we become ashamed of our bodies, self-conscious of every seeming imperfection, and prefer to hide them. We become more focused on our external persona than the essence within. The same happens with our soul. We fear that expressions of our soul will be denigrated in this physical realm, and so we try to keep them hidden and repressed. We recognize our soulful expressions as manifestations of our most pure and truest self and feel vulnerable when we allow others to see them.

Guitar players develop callouses on their fingers. This is necessary to protect one's fingertips from the guitar's strings. Without them, fingers become painfully raw and playing guitar becomes a torturous experience. Every so often, the callouses grow too thick to feel the strings, however, and must be reduced in thickness by filing or picking them off. Guitar players seek a balance between protection and the need to feel the strings. Well-adjusted poets and artists find ways to express their deepest responses to the world while guarding against unhealthy or excessive exposures. These are possible metaphors for the balance we seek in exposing our beautiful soul. The soul wants to express and experience life in all of its raw, physical beauty, but it must at least partially shelter itself from the physical pain that can result from such vulnerability.

A powerful example of a soul seeking to connect deeply with other souls is found in the life of Jesus of Nazareth. He consistently ignored the social and religious conventions that did not encourage soulful expressions. He criticized rules and regulations that served no purpose other than to keep oppressed people oppressed. He sought to free people from that which kept them trapped in their material existence, saying, "for where your treasure is, there your heart will be also."[14] Even as he was dying on the cross, he asked God to forgive his executioners because they did not know what they were doing. When we deny

---

[14] Matthew 6:21

the expressions of our beautiful soul, we do not know what we deny to ourselves and others.

Again, in the words of Don McLean from his song *Vincent*, "They would not listen, they did not know how..."[15] The fact is that we cannot understand or appreciate a soul's beautiful expressions unless we allow those expressions to connect with and move us in our deepest being. Only in such moments of shared vulnerability can a connection be established that allows us to hear and appreciate the unearthly beauty of a soulful embodiment.

---

[15] Don McLean, *Vincent.* Universal Music Publishing Group, 1970.

Chapter 21

A Beautiful Soul, Part 3

I do not call you servants any longer, because the servant does not know what the master is doing; but I have called you friends, because I have made known to you everything that I have heard from my Father. John 15:15

On the one hand, our soul needs to express in physical ways. On the other hand, our soul is not of this world, but is an extension of God's eternal realm. As such, we can feel wounded when a sincere expression of our deepest essence is not received with the same level of respect and care from which it came.

One of the hardest things to grasp is that we are quite literally one at the soul level – one with God and one with each other. An indication of how much we identify with our physical nature is in how much we feel separate from others. The truth is that we sink or swim together. When others suffer, we suffer, regardless of whether we feel the direct impact that tragedies across the globe have on us. This is why Jesus of Nazareth and other great spiritual leaders manifested as suffering servants. They knew who they were at their core, and so they recognized the suffering of the world as their own suffering. Author and teacher, Richard Rohr, writes, "Becoming who we really are is a matter of learning how to become more and more deeply connected."[16]

Because the soul is not bound by time and space, our connections with others are not limited by time and space, either. That is how we can maintain a close friendship with someone whom we seldom see and pick up conversations from where we left off years before. It is why we can be moved to tears by a symphony written centuries ago by a composer we never knew personally. It explains why certain paintings of long-dead artists can connect so intimately and emotionally with something deep inside of us. These connections are soul-to-soul and they spring from a realm beyond the physical. The concept of *soul mates* has been hijacked by romantic notions, but it really refers to deep connections with others that transcend space and time. Truly, our soul knows no boundaries.

I attended a presentation by a poet in college. He drew a distinct line between those who opened a channel to their soul for others to experience and those who did not. In his opinion, there were two choices – live life as an emotionally unstable but serious artist or live life as a stable but mediocre (at best) artist. In my opinion, this particular poet probably succeeded on the emotionally unstable front, but I found his poetry to be more an expression of his egoic insecurities than reflections of

---

[16] Richard Rohr, *Near Occasions of Grace*. Maryknoll, NY: Orbis Books, 1993.

something terribly profound or deep. I do not believe our choices for manifesting the spiritual, soulful part of ourselves to be nearly so stark. In fact, I believe we are meant to allow our souls to embody in all the ways we are gifted to manifest. With an awareness that not everyone will receive our soulful expressions with the appreciation and respect we believe they deserve, we can learn to express from the deepest parts of our being simply for the joy of such expression.

Our ego becomes overly identified with our mortal bodies and with the opinions of others. It is our ego that is fragile and easily wounded, not our soul. When we overly identify with our ego and with our physical being, we will almost certainly turn into an emotional basket case, like the poet mentioned

When the veil between the physical and spiritual begins to thin, we can allow our beautiful soul to shine through and touch others.

earlier, anytime anything that springs from our essence is rejected. As we learn to identify more with the eternal, spiritual part of us we are less likely to be wounded by the words and actions of others.

When the veil between the physical and spiritual begins to thin, we can allow our beautiful soul to shine through and touch others. This is evangelism without words. We allow others to be touched by the Spirit through us. Whether we manifest great works of art, poetry, music, or just comforting presence is beside the point. Our beautiful soul will draw out the beauty in others, and there is no art form more beautiful or impactful than that. This is how we manifest the healing presence of God; it brings the peace that passes understanding. It is how we live our lives to the fullest, beautiful body *and* beautiful soul.

Chapter 22

Gods I Do Not Believe In

Fools think their own way is right... Proverbs 12:15a

When joining the First United Methodist Church in Lawrence, Kansas, shortly after getting married, my wife and I attended an orientation class with the Senior Pastor, Virgil Brady. He explained that United Methodists believe and worship in many different ways. He had a pad of newsprint on an easel and wrote, "God…" He said, "Methodists believe in God, but they believe in God in many different ways." Then he wrote, "Jesus…" He said, "Methodists believe in Jesus, but they also believe in different ways about Jesus." In other words, the United Methodist church is united in its belief in God and Jesus, but allows a lot of leeway in terms of what that means to its individual members.

I have thought about those words many times in the decades since that orientation. For me, it is sometimes easier to articulate what I do not believe about God than it is to articulate what I do believe.

While I believe God loves us in spite of our beliefs, here are a few descriptors of gods I do not believe in:

1. *A God who punishes.* I do not believe in a God who punishes us for our wrongdoing. Rather, our wrongdoing creates its own punishment. Some may appear to get away with bad behavior because the law of cause and effect does not always bring the effect immediately after the cause. It is the brilliant way God created the world that makes our actions automatically hurt when they are inconsistent with the common good. We learn best by being broken, but God does not do the breaking. Rather, God stands beside us in our suffering, lifting us out of our despair. God does not, however, intervene between us and the consequences of our own choices.
2. *A God who discriminates.* I do not believe in a God who excludes certain groups of people because of their ethnicity, religious practices, sexual orientation, gender, race, or their choices of profession. We see this very clearly in Jesus, who excluded no one. In fact, Jesus specifically reached out to the outcasts, downtrodden, and forgotten souls of society – the prostitutes, the lepers, the tax collectors, the disabled, and the foreigners. He treated women and children as equals in a deeply patriarchal society. Given the life that Jesus lived, I cannot believe a God who accepted all in Jesus would exclude anyone because they did not say the right words, practice the right

religion, or behave according to certain humanly-determined norms.

3. *A God who prospers believers with prestige, power, and possessions.* Some Christians believe God rewards good behavior with prestigious positions, lavishing the chosen with luxurious possessions. It is so contrary to the life of Jesus that it hardly warrants mention here. If anything, it is our obsession with power, prestige, and possessions that creates the spiritual obstacles that trip up many of us, particularly in the West. We seek security and riches in all the wrong places because the wealth and blessing of God is not found in earthly materiality. Humility and brokenness are what make God apparent in our lives (see Matthew 5:3-12).

4. *An old, white, bearded man.* This image of God comes more from artists' depictions of God than from anything written in scripture. It is no surprise that in the patriarchal times of the authors of the Bible God would be portrayed as male, but a God of all must be beyond gender, race, and physical appearance. God loves God's creation in its entirety (including, but not exclusive to old, white men).

The important point is not how we picture God but that we are open to the connection with God from our end.

These are a few of the gods I no longer believe in and do not find helpful in seeking the God of the Universe. I respect those who may treasure these and other similar images of God, however. God comes to all of us in ways unique and specific to our nature. The important point is not how we picture God but that we are open to the connection with God from our end. Anything short of that, at least for me, is like praying with one eye open in that our beliefs limit what we are willing to accept as God's nature.

Chapter 23

Divine Violence, Part 1

Let burning coals fall on them! Let them be flung into pits, no more to rise! Psalm 140:10

There are a number of methods to interpret what we read in the Bible and other sacred texts. One common method, although it is relatively recent in Christian history, is the *literal* interpretation. This assumes that God *dictated* the Bible as opposed to *inspiring* it, as Timothy states in his Epistle.[17] "It is in the Bible, therefore God said it, so I believe it," is a common sentiment of those who apply a literal interpretation. Others follow a *historical* reading, meaning they see the Bible as a historical record that may or may not have current relevance beyond recording events from long ago. Another method of interpretation is the *allegorical* or *metaphorical,* which bypasses questions of factuality and seeks the *story-within-the-story* the reading attempts to impart. For example, Jesus used *parables* in his teaching, which are

---

[17] See 2 Timothy 3:16.

not factual accounts but are relatable stories with an important moral lesson. There is a use for each type of interpretation, depending on the scripture passage and our stage in life, but I find the metaphorical reading most useful for spiritual growth and understanding.

One concern that turns many away from the Bible is the violence recorded, requested, and alluded to throughout its pages. Particularly for those who read the Bible literally, God appears to play favorites and sometimes violently so. For example, as the Israelites were seeking their freedom from slavery,

> *One concern that turns many away from the Bible is the violence recorded, requested, and alluded to throughout its pages.*

God caused a series of plagues to fall upon the people of Egypt in order to convince Pharaoh to grant them their freedom. The tenth plague brought death to all the firstborn in Egypt, both children and livestock.[18] As a firstborn myself, I find this very disconcerting! Not only were the plagues caused by God, but God purposely hardened Pharaoh's heart following the previous plagues so that Pharaoh would not set the Israelites free.[19] A literal reading of Exodus would mean that God not only caused thousands of deaths to innocent people and animals to send a message to Pharaoh, but God was manipulating Pharaoh in such

---

[18] Exodus 12:29.
[19] See Exodus 11:10.

a way as to prevent him from relinquishing. One must be a nimble biblical apologist to reconcile the literal Biblical record with what we want to believe is a loving and just God.

In the creation story of Genesis, after creating every living thing on the earth, God created humankind and pronounced the *whole of creation* "very good."[20] This story does not distinguish the Israelites as better than non-Israelites, although much of the Bible refers to them as God's "chosen" race (never mind that most of the Bible was written by these chosen ones). My point is that a God who created all things and all peoples and pronounced them "very good" seems unlikely to take sides in squabbles among God's creation, let alone initiate or support such violent and fatal action against either side. The Psalms are full of accounts of exactly that sort of vicious favoritism, either requested by someone feeling offended or granted on their behalf. My belief is that God's part in these stories is either a misunderstanding on the part of the author or an allegorical truth-sharing using a non-factual story.

Fortunately, there is another way to understand such texts without portraying God as arbitrary or violent toward innocents. As followers of Jesus, who was unquestionably non-violent, we need another option. A metaphorical reading, while not taking a position on the literal or historical accuracy of the passages, leads one to ponder how the message applies to one's own life. For example, we can read the story of the exodus as the story of our own struggle to free the true and pure part of ourselves

---

[20] Genesis 1:31.

from the ego-self and its bondage to materialism. Pharaoh represents our ego, and the Israelites are our true self. The various plagues represent the numerous attempts we make to free ourselves from the addictive consumer-mentality of our culture. There are many plagues because we must persist with sustained efforts at self-change. The death of the first-born can represent the "death" of some of our "first-born" ideas about life and God that are either wrong or that we have outgrown, many of which we inherit from ancestors. Those ideas and beliefs can be stubborn entities, like Pharaoh, that do not easily relent.

Such metaphorical, internal violence is one thing. The very real and tragic violence in our world is quite another. I will reflect on that in the next chapter.

Chapter 24

Divine Violence, Part 2

For it is from within, from the human heart, that evil intentions come... Mark 7:21a

We can read the violent sections of the Bible in a metaphorical way that helps us reconcile a loving God with a sometimes violent text. This method of biblical interpretation is based on the foundational belief that our inner struggles not only mirror the violence recorded in the Bible, but also mirror the external violence we witness in our world today. These inner struggles occur between our ego-self – the part of us that is overly identified with our mortal, physical being – and our true-self – the part of us that is inseparably wedded to God, others, and the eternal. These two *selves,* both of which are us, find themselves in frequent conflict because their goals, values, and perspectives differ widely. Unfortunately, the violence in our world is not metaphorical. The murder of innocents, physical abuse, oppression, and the heartbroken victims and families left in their wake are all very real.

Let me restate the proposition that some will find

silly or heretical: The world *outside* of our selves mirrors the world *inside* of our selves. As such, our eternal fate is inseparably tied to that of all others. Salvation is not an individual achievement; rather, it is a communal awakening. The traditional view of heaven would not be heaven if we were there alone. That would be hell. We have neither the wisdom nor the perspective to judge who is worthy of either glory or damnation. What we have is a commandment to love each other. Followers of Jesus, by definition, try

---

We have neither the wisdom nor the perspective to judge who is worthy of either glory or damnation. What we have is a commandment to love each other.

---

to do what he did. Jesus reached out to and served those on the margins of society – prostitutes, tax collectors, widows and orphans, the sick and lame, immigrants, the blind. In no uncertain terms he told us to go and do likewise. This command was not simply because loving these people is a nice thing to do, but because *bringing them into our circle of care is a necessary step for our own entry into the kingdom of heaven.* Remember, our inner life mirrors what we witness externally as their lives.

A common question I hear in discussions of mass tragedies like the Holocaust is this: *Where was God?* That question is as wrong as it is reasonable. We are far too quick to blame God for evil manifestations of human brokenness and ignorance. The correct question is: *Where were we?* Granted, most of us were not alive during the Holocaust, but where are we with the immigrants at our southern border? Where are we in the mass shootings occurring throughout our country? Where are we in human trafficking and the myriad of other continuing forms of human slavery and oppression? If we are God's hands and feet on earth, *where are we?* We are an integral part of the fabric of this society and the communities where we live. We help perpetuate that which we do not oppose. What public action have I taken on gun control, global hunger, immigration, or human trafficking? Personally, I have done far too little.

So here is our dilemma: If the outer world mirrors our inner world, what are we doing about the senseless violence within? I think the answer begins with the degree to which we consciously identify with our ego self. The ego has no problem with personal gain at the expense of another. It has no problem looking the other way when someone else is being beaten or robbed, as long as the perpetrator does not come after it. Is it any wonder we live in a violent, self-centered society? The ego has no social conscience, and a lack of social responsibility is at the heart of mass human tragedies. Assuming personal responsibility for the suffering of others is lacking. The ego is very quick to assign blame elsewhere. And the first to suffer and last to recover are those at the margins – the ones to whom Jesus dedicated his ministry.

Once we identify more strongly with our true self, our connection to others becomes more apparent. We can no longer stand by and witness the persecution of others because *their* persecution is *our* persecution. Refusing to consider scripture and the life around us as a reflection of our inner world is like praying with one eye open. We allow into our awareness only those parts of reality that support our ego-self. And those at the margins pay the price for our ignorance.

Chapter 25

Divine Violence, Part 3

His disciples asked him, "Rabbi, who sinned, this man or his parents, that he was born blind? Jesus answered, "Neither this man nor his parents sinned; he was born blind so that God's works might be revealed in him. We must work the words of him who sent me while it is day; night is coming when no one can work. John 9:2-4

As a way to illustrate the shared responsibility for the violence manifesting in our world as mass shootings, human slavery, and various forms of oppression and abuse, consider a sometimes-violent, homeless, and mentally ill man living on the streets of our town. Whose fault is it that he is homeless? We are quick to blame local governments for their inadequate funding for affordable housing. Whose fault is it that he has untreated mental illness? We are quick to blame the government's inadequate funding for mental health services. Whose fault is it that he is sometimes violent? We are quick to blame the local justice system. Now, follow this chain: Who controls governmental purse strings and priorities? (Our elected officials) Who elects these officials? (We do)

Most elected officials are inundated with complaints about high government spending. Others complain that taxes need to increase to take care of people like this man, but they believe *someone else's* taxes should increase. We recognize the need, but not our own responsibility to participate in the solution.

So, who is to blame for this homeless, mentally ill man on our streets? Is it the government, local service providers, elected officials, or the voters? The responsibility for the problem and the solution, of course, rests on all of us. I do not point this out to infuse guilt. This is *shared* guilt and *shared* responsibility. It starts, however, with recognizing and taking responsibility for our individual contribution to the problem. Pope Francis, in his message for the

> *Solutions to societal problems begin with recognizing and taking responsibility for our individual contribution to the problem*

2017 World Day of Peace said, "Jesus taught that the true battlefield, where violence and peace meet, is the human heart: for 'it is from within, from the human heart, that evil intentions come' (Mark 7:21)."[21] The change we seek begins within. As I noted previously, the external violence in our world mirrors the internal violence within each of us. Our desire to shift the responsibility for society's ills onto others is a

---

[21] Pope Francis, "Nonviolence: A Style of Politics for Peace," Message of His Holiness Pope Francis for the Celebration of the Fiftieth World Day of Peace (January 1, 2017).

manifestation of that violence. It reveals the split between our true self, which suffers with the suffering, and our ego-self, which focuses narrowly on its own self-interest.

How do we identify and heal the violence within so we can begin healing the violence we witness in our world? Here are a few suggestions:

1. *Identify the areas of internal resistance, the motives and beliefs, inhibiting your ability to recognize society's problems as your problems.* For example, "My taxes are already too high" or "That is not my responsibility."
2. *Once exposed, work to transform those motives and beliefs from something individually focused to something more socially focused.* For example, transform the belief that "my taxes are too high" to "we are all going to have to sacrifice to resolve this issue."
3. *Form or join like-minded people to influence positive change in your community as a whole.* For example, form a group to pressure local officials and voters to adequately and sustainably fund local services for the marginalized.

The essential nature of sin is the sense of separation from others. Many perpetrators of human atrocities are isolated beings trapped in their isolated ego-self. How can we safely and effectively integrate those on the margins into society? How can we expand our boundaries to make them feel included? How can we give them a sense of belonging and social responsibility?

In today's scripture, the followers of Jesus wanted to know who was responsible for a man being born blind. In his day, many believed the man's blindness was due either to his or his parent's sin. Jesus said the man was born blind to reveal God's works – works performed by the hands and hearts of those seeking to love God actively in the world. Whose fault is it we live in a violent world? Ultimately, it is ours. For what purpose? Perhaps it is so those willing to be the hands and heart of God on earth can manifest God's glory by transforming divine violence into divine love. That is how we will open the gates to God's kingdom on earth.

Chapter 26

Praying With Both Eyes Closed

But as for me, my prayer is to you, O Lord. At an acceptable time, O God, in the abundance of your steadfast love, answer me. Psalm 69:13

I began this book with a reflection about praying with one eye open. I used it as a metaphor for not giving oneself fully to God. Since that time I have written numerous additional reflections about the various ways we find to avoid or otherwise not surrender to God as much as we can or perhaps should. Make no mistake, I do not write these as a person who is particularly good at that type of surrender. Maybe that makes me a hypocrite, but these are topics I struggle with and assume at least some others do, too. I remember Sundays in church as a child during prayer time looking around the sanctuary for people whose eyes were not closed. I always found a few. I think I figured if I got caught, the captor would automatically expose his or her own guilt if he or she called me out. It was not that I was serving as the *prayer police* as much as it was just difficult for me to keep both eyes closed during the prayers that seemed to drag on forever. I, like most of us, was taught to pray with both eyes closed. I guess it was considered disrespectful to God to be looking around during prayer.

The years have given me a slightly different perspective on prayer. I no longer believe God cares whether our eyes are open or closed. I do, however, believe it can make a difference to our personal experience of prayer. We receive so much information and stimulation through our eyes that it is difficult, if not impossible, to focus on something

---

I do not believe God cares whether our eyes are open or closed in prayer. I do, however, believe it can make a difference to our personal experience of prayer.

---

ephemeral, like God, with our eyes open. We believe our connection to God is internal and, as such, that our *gaze* should be internal, too. That implies that our eyes should be closed.

As I have stated in earlier chapters, having both eyes closed makes us vulnerable. We cannot see what is going on around us. We do not know but that everyone else might be staring at something that has gone weirdly wrong with our hair. Keeping our eyes open is probably an instinctual trait dating back to the days when we needed to watch for angry Mastodons that might be coming after us. Keeping our eyes open helps us keep control of our environment, or at least gives us a sense of control. Which is exactly *not* the point in prayer. Closing our eyes requires a degree of trust and surrender, both of which are helpful orientations in seeking God's presence. In my experience, God does not compete for our attention.

There is a school of thought that when we are doing something, we should be focused on that one thing to the exclusion of everything else. Work efficiency experts tell us to clear everything out of the visual field in our work space except for the immediate task at hand. Distractions like phone calls, emails, and other projects begging for attention come at a cost in terms of getting our tasks done in a timely and accurate manner. Experts tell us we cannot multi-task nearly as well as we believe, so attending to one task at a time is preferable. Under this methodology, when we pray, we should be completely focused on our prayer, and our eyes should be closed.

Certainly in our relationships, when a friend or partner is speaking, particularly about something sensitive, we want to give our attention wholly to her or him. A quick and sure way to damage the relationship is to check our cell phone while the partner is sharing something close to her or his heart. It is a colossal show of disrespect and an indication of how little we value what is important to him or her.

Perhaps for all these reasons and more, keeping both eyes closed during prayer is the best option. It helps keep us focused on God (at least in theory), and it puts us in an attitude of surrender. Having both eyes closed is a symbolic way of saying we trust God to protect us in our times of vulnerability. Those of us who are parents want our children to trust and feel safe in our presence, so why would God feel differently?

Chapter 27

Praying With One Eye Open (Reprise)

Devote yourselves to prayer, keeping alert in it with Thanksgiving. At the same time pray for us as well...
Colossians 4:2-3a

Throughout this book I have presented the metaphor of praying with one eye open in a negative light. I have used it as an illustration of how we hold back from surrendering completely to God. There is another way of looking at this in which praying with one eye open might actually be the most appropriate way to pray. First, I'll take a slight, but hopefully interesting and enlightening detour.

Most people are aware that our brains have two hemispheres. It is how we and much of the animal kingdom were created. In very broad terms, the left hemisphere specializes in small details and attempts to categorize what it experiences into concrete groupings of right or wrong, dark or light, male or female. The left hemisphere, useful and necessary as it is, cannot see the *big picture*. The right hemisphere specializes in the big picture and attempts to fit its experiences into a larger whole. It seeks similarities and relationships, not differences. Here is an example of the typical functioning of the two hemispheres of the brain, paraphrased from Iain McGilchrist's book, *The Master and His Emissary*[22]:

> A small bird in search of food must perform two tasks simultaneously. First, he/she must focus narrowly on the ground to identify what is edible from what is inedible, i.e., a grain of wheat from a pebble. This is detail work that is the domain of the left hemisphere, which controls the right eye. So our bird is scanning the ground with its right eye in search of food. At the same time, our little friend must also scan the environment for predators. This bigger picture focus is the domain of the right hemisphere, so the bird is also checking her/his surroundings with the left eye. For its well-being, our bird must focus *simultaneously* on its internal needs and its external protection.

You may wonder what this has to do with praying with one eye open. I use it to illustrate the dual nature of our earthly lives. Although we are one being, we have both a spiritual and physical aspect to that being. In a related way, we have an internal life as well as the life going on around us. Our divided brains show how we were created with the ability to

---

[22] Iain McGilchrist, *The Master and His Emissary*. Yale University Press, 2019.

comprehend and experience in both detailed and broad ways, in concrete and ethereal realms. In addition, as we awaken to the true nature of our being, we are capable of unifying and reconciling what we witness in the world around us with the life we experience within.

In prayer, there is a need to focus on the details of our personal situation and a simultaneous need to be aware of the needs of others around us. Like the hungry little bird, we have need for both attention to present details and a view beyond our inner world. For prayer to be effective, we must be aware of both our internal and external worlds.

When we understand that God created us with physical eyes and senses to perceive the world around us, but also with internal senses to explore our inner lives, then we begin to see the wisdom and practicality

---

In prayer, there is a need to focus on the details of our personal situation and a simultaneous need to be aware of the needs of others around us.

---

of praying with one eye open. In other words, we have been given the capacity to be attuned to our inner and outer worlds simultaneously. Even if we close our physical eyes in prayer, we cannot turn a blind eye to the needs and sufferings of those around us. Likewise, we cannot ignore the struggles and conflicts within, pretending as if they do not exist. Our inner and outer worlds *mirror* one another and ignoring one simply intensifies the struggle in the other.

We were created as single beings with a dual nature. We actually can attend to seemingly opposite realities and see how they are two sides of the same thing. We were created to be *unifiers,* both of our inner and outer worlds. This is the peace of Christ when we can embrace all the diverse realities in this life as a single creation, valuable and worthy of our respect and love simply by being a part of this amazing creation. In order to grow into the knowledge of our essential unity, we probably need to pray with one eye closed and one eye open.

Appendix A

Intro to Centering Prayer

"...But when you pray, go to your inner room, close the door and pray to your Father in secret. And your Father, who sees in secret, will reward you." Matthew 6:6

Centering prayer is participation in God's first language, which is *silence*. It seeks to move us from a one-way, spoken conversation to God to a wordless communion with God. It is not a replacement for spoken prayer, but it should deepen the prayer experience.

In Centering Prayer we *consent* to God's will; our *intent* is solely to be in the presence of God as we *surrender* to what is. We carry no expectations into the prayer, except to be in the presence of God. We are not looking for answers, healings, revelations, or inspirations.

During the prayer, thoughts will arise, but strive not to attach to them. Allow them to come and go as they will. Be gentle, patient, and subtle, as if holding a sleeping baby. Attempt to move your attention from the chatter in your head into a silent and open experience in the heart.

Centering Prayer Guidelines (drawn heavily from the work of Fr. Thomas Keating and Contemplative Outreach)

1. Choose a "sacred word" (see explanation below) as the symbol of your intention to consent to God's presence and action within.
2. Sitting comfortably and with eyes closed, settle briefly and silently introduce the sacred word as the symbol of your consent to God's presence and action within.
3. When engaged with your thoughts, return ever-so-gently to the sacred word.
4. At the end of the prayer period, remain in silence with eyes closed for a couple of minutes.

If you become too physically or emotionally uncomfortable during the prayer, quietly open your eyes. Gently stretch or walk around if necessary.

A word about the Sacred Word

The sacred word is a *symbol* of our intent to consent. The word itself is not sacred – our intent is what is sacred. It should be no more than one or two syllables. Some possible examples include God, Jesus, Abba, Father, Mother, Mary, Amen, Love, Peace, Listen, Mercy, Let Go, Be Still, Silence, Stillness, Faith, Trust. Stick with the same word throughout a prayer session.

Centering Prayer Practice

The standard recommendation is for two, 20 minute centering prayer sessions daily. The benefits of Centering Prayer are often not experienced during the prayer itself but in our daily life following a commitment to its regular practice.

Centering Prayer Resources

www.contemplativeoutreach.com

<u>Centering Prayer, a 40 Day Practice</u>.
Contemplative Outreach.

www.Gravitycenter.com

Thomas Keating, <u>Intimacy with God</u>. Crossroad Publishing. 2015.

Cynthia Bourgeault, <u>Centering Prayer and Inner Awakening</u>. Cowley. 2004.

Appendix B

Walking Meditation

"People usually consider walking on water or in thin air a miracle. But I think the real miracle is not to walk either on water or in thin air, but to walk on earth. Every day we are engaged in a miracle which we don't even recognize: a blue sky, white clouds, green leaves, the black, curious eyes of a child – our own two eyes. All is a miracle."[23] Thich Nhat Hahn

1. **Grounding**
    a. Standing or sitting, begin with 1-3 minutes of silence.
    b. Draw your attention to the breeze, the sun on your skin, the sounds around you, and the weight of your body against the earth.
2. **Preparation**
    a. Warm up by stretching slowly and rolling your feet.
    b. Move at your own pace. Rest when needed.
    c. Pause, listen, be open.
    d. Allow thoughts to come and go as you move.

---

[23] https://www.goodreads.com/quotes/5022-people-usually-consider-walking-on-water-or-in-thin-air

3. **Movement**
    a. Allow yourself to simply be present to your body and how it moves.
    b. Feel your feet as they move along the earth.
    c. Notice the casual swing of your arms.
    d. Be patient and unhurried.
    e. Allow your curiosity to guide you as you are present to what is around you.
    f. Listen to the sounds of your heartbeat, your breathing, and your steps.
4. **Transformation**
    a. As you walk, shift your awareness to the Divine Presence in all of creation.
    b. See the Indwelling Presence of the Divine as you gaze upon yourself, those around you, and all of creation.
    c. Be fully present to Love. Let each step remind you that we walk in Love.
5. **Closing**
    a. End with a moment of silence and gratitude.
    b. Consider sharing your experience with friends.

Walking Meditation Resources:

www.walk2connect.com

Appendix C

Intro to *Lectio Divina*

Lectio Divina (Lex'-ee-oh Dah-vee'-nah) means *sacred reading*. It is a centuries-old method of praying the scriptures and other sacred texts. It is not a read-through-the-Bible-in-one-year type of program. Rather, it requires slow, deliberate reading of relatively short passages, taking time to place oneself into the story and listening for God's personal message to us in it. For 1500+ years, Benedictine monks have practiced this method of study and prayer as a part of their daily routine.

There are at least a couple of different ways to practice *Lectio Divina*, but probably more important than the method used is getting into a rhythm of regular practice, daily if possible. A morning and evening session is optimal for those able to do so.

A couple of foundational principles for either of the two methods I outline below are as follows:

1. Do not randomly select passages for study. For example, select a book of the Bible, start with the first chapter and continue to the end of that book. It is not unusual to spend months with a single book. Another option is to use the daily Lectionary, which will jump around throughout the Bible, but the verses

you study will not be random or self-determined.
2. Read slowly and aloud, if possible. We process information differently when we hear words than when we read them silently. One goal of *Lectio Divina* is to absorb the sacred text into our body and heart centers. Reading aloud enhances that process.

With these shared traits in mind, here are two methods of *Lectio Divina:*

Lectio Divina, Method 1: Read, Reflect, Respond, Rest

1. After selecting a short passage for study (for example, a single paragraph), sit in a quiet place with minimal distractions. Say a short prayer of anticipation.
2. *Read* your selection slowly and aloud. Stop and consider what you have read. Return to any word or phrase that may have caught your attention. What about that word or phrase attracted or repelled you?
3. Read your selection a second time, slowly and aloud. *Reflect* on what speaks to you from the reading. Perhaps assume a role in the story. What do you see, hear, smell, or feel?
4. Read your selection a third time, slowly and aloud. *Respond* to what you have read. Perhaps offer a prayer or ponder what the reading suggests about your life. Journal your thoughts if you desire.
5. Read your selection a fourth time, slowly and aloud. *Rest* in God's presence.

6. Close your practice with a short prayer of gratitude.

Lectio Divina, Method 2

1. Determine a timeframe for your practice. You might begin with a 20 minute session.
2. Sitting in a quiet place with limited distractions, say a short prayer of anticipation.
3. Begin reading your selected passage, slowly and aloud. Continue reading until a word, phrase, or thought grabs your attention. Stop to reflect on that word, phrase or thought, perhaps journaling whatever insights arise.
4. Continue reading, pausing to reflect and journal if and when something speaks to you, until your selected time is up.
5. Close your practice with a short prayer of gratitude.

Praying With One Eye Open

About the Author

Greg Hildenbrand lives south of Lawrence, Kansas with his wife, Carrie. They have two adult children, Grace and Reid. Greg is a volunteer leader of blended worship at First United Methodist Church in Lawrence. He is a graduate of the Living School at the Center for Action and Contemplation. His weekly blog, *Life Notes*, podcasts, many of his songs, and information about his books and CDs, are available at www.ContemplatingGrace.com.

Praying With One Eye Open

Made in the USA
Coppell, TX
09 November 2019